WELCOME TO OUR GARDEN

The *Elegance* French Wire ribbons which we've use... romantic history. They come from Lyon, the center o... Renowned for their haute couture fabrics and hand wo... Lyonnaise artisans have been creating beautiful ribbons ... generations. This labor-intensive industry is still based on the same technology used 100 years ago. Each loom can weave only four of the wider ribbons at a time, and most of the ribbon mills have been in the same families for centuries. Today's artisans take the same care and pride in their work as did their grandfathers.

Vintage fashions and all kinds of needlework are passions we both share. We were intrigued by the ribbon flowers which have been a part of so many works of textile art - ruched dahlias peering out of a basket in the center of a Baltimore Album Quilt, velvet pansies languishing on the bodice of a fin-de-siecle evening gown, satin roses cascading down a Poiret skirt, a black cloche hat nearly buried under a bevy of black-eyed susans. Old books and magazines presented many ideas for using ribbon flowers, but the instructions were minimal.

We took classes, practiced, experimented and simply played with the ribbons. And in the end, the ribbons themselves seduced us with their glowing rainbow of colors and luminous shading. We think you'll enjoy them too!

Diane & Bonnie

CONTENTS

SIZING THEM UP

French Ribbon widths are labelled by a number, rather than an inch width. You may find that there is some variation in the width of ribbons woven by different manufacturers on different looms.

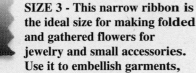

SIZE 3 - This narrow ribbon is the ideal size for making folded and gathered flowers for jewelry and small accessories. Use it to embellish garments, for small-scale crazy piecing, or in silk ribbon embroidery. While it's the best size for triple-loop leaves and simple rosettes, #3 ribbon can be a bit fiddly to sew into tiny cupped or prairie point leaves. These tiny leaves are a unique accent for silk ribbon embroidery.

SIZE 5 - Flowers and leaves made from this size ribbon can be the larger ones in groupings for small accessories. #5 is a good size for embellishing garments without overwhelming them. Even if your project calls for mostly large flowers, a few #5 blossoms will fill in the gaps and offer a refreshing change in scale.

SIZE 9 - This ribbon is available in the widest range of colors and styles. It is an easy width for beginners to handle, and it produces realistically-scaled flowers. So make your first flowers and leaves from #9; then try the narrower ribbons. Make most of your leaves from #9 ribbon because they are the best-sized leaves for filling in the background.

SIZE 12 - This wide ribbon is great for longer leaves and double rosettes. The larger flowers make ideal embellishments for a large Baltimore-style quilt or a wreath for your mantel or door.

RAISING YOUR RIBBON I.Q.

All the ribbons used in this book are Quilters' Resource Inc.'s *Elegance* French Wired Ribbons. We'd like to introduce you to some of our favorites. The most likely place to find them is in specialty fabric, needlework , quilt shops and better flower shops. Don't pass up the solids when shopping for ribbons. Satins, dobbies, failles and moirés will add texture to flowers and leaves.

CROSS DYED
In cross dyed ribbons, the warp threads (or lengthwise threads) are one color and the weft threads (or cross threads) are another. The result is an iridescent look, which shows up beautifully when the ribbon is gathered and folded.

OMBRÉ
Some ombré ribbons are monochromatic, shading from light to dark pink, for example, while others change hue, perhaps going from green to violet or yellow to rose. The warp threads of an ombré ribbon change color from one selvedge to the other, while the weft threads are all one color. Ombré Noir is a rich looking ombré ribbon with dark weft threads.

OVERDYED
Created by starting with an ombré ribbon and then printing changing shades of color along the length, overdyed ribbons are the most colorful of all the woven ribbons. It's possible to make at least four very differently-colored flowers or leaves from each ribbon.

SERGE
Woven in a twill weave, the diagonal lines running across serge ribbons add a unique texture. They are available in solid and ombré versions. Because they tend to ravel a bit more than plain-woven ribbons, handle them gently and add an extra 1/2" when cutting.

ORGANDY
The French have developed this new, sheer ribbon with a slightly sparkly look. The Ombré versions have an airier look than regular ombrés.

SHADY CHARACTERS

Ombré & overdyed ribbons are chameleon-like in the way they shade from one edge to the other or change color along the length. It's like having two or more ribbons with which to work.

Ombré ribbons can become two very different-looking flowers.

Ruched flower with dark shade on the outer edge of the petals.

Ruched flower with light shade on the outer edge of petals.

One Ombré ribbon results in two shades of leaves.

Dark leaves.

Lighter leaves.

Ribbons with one green edge are versatile.

With the green edge out, they are ideal for leaves.

Make flowers by gathering the green edge into the center.

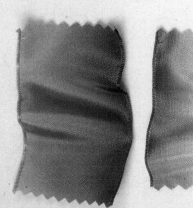

The technique you choose can affect the look of your flowers.

Folded roses are two-tone. Overdyed ribbons are very effective when folded.

Gathered roses can be either light or dark, depending on which edge is gathered.

BASICS TRAINING

NEEDLES

We recommend a Milliners size 9 or 10 needle, sometimes referred to as a Straw Needle. Milliners have traditionally used them to sew trims onto hats. Milliners needles have the same size eye and shaft as a Sharps but are much longer. The extra length allows you to gather more fabric onto the needle when ruching. It also makes it easier to sew the completed flowers to the backing.

THREAD

Fine nylon beading thread is strong enough for long rows of gathering or ruching stitches. It won't break when you give it that extra tug to pull the centers together. We like size 23 beading thread, which is generally available in white and black. You can also use quilting thread or Nymo nylon thread. Regular sewing thread in colors to match the ribbon is fine for stitching flowers and leaves to crinoline.

CRINOLINE

This stiff woven fabric looks a lot like needlepoint canvas. It can be found in most fabric stores and comes in white and black. Use a small piece of the lightest weight to tack down gathered roses. Stitch the groupings of flowers and leaves to the crinoline, then tack the crinoline to your garment. It will then be easy to remove the groupings for cleaning. Heavier buckram or leftover scraps of closely woven needlepoint canvas (size 22 or 24) are ideal backings for projects such as pins, which need a more substantial base.

PINS

Stock up on extra long 1 1/2" to 2" pins with large heads for securely pinning down the flowers and leaves before sewing. We like the Clover Flower Head pins because they are long, thin, and sharp, and their heads don't get lost among the flowers.

SCISSORS

We've never damaged a pair of scissors cutting the wires in French Ribbon, but the wires may be more substantial in other ribbons. It's important to cut the ribbon cleanly, so set aside your very best fabric scissors and sharpen up your second best as backups.

NEEDLE NOSE OR JEWELER'S PLIERS

These are not a necessity, unless you have weak hands or long fingernails. Use them to grasp and pull the ribbon wires

TAILOR'S AWL

The long thin tip of an awl is helpful for pushing the ribbon edges where you want them. The pointed end of a paint brush also works well

RIBBON

It's a good idea to begin by purchasing at least three different brands of wire-edged ribbon, both French & American. This will allow you to see how the texture, colors, and shading vary and which types are the easiest to work with.

You will find that it's wise to buy the best quality ribbon you can afford. Fine ribbon, like Quilters' Resource Inc.' s *Elegance* French Ribbon, is woven from superior quality fibers and has an extremely high thread count. The result is a soft ribbon with a gorgeous, subtle shading. The extra fine copper wire is very flexible and will not tarnish with age.

A STARTING ASSORTMENT OF COLORS AND SIZES

Start with a range of sizes. Size 9 is the easiest to manipulate. Make your first practice flowers from it; then work your way down to the narrower sizes.

SIZES

# 3	1 yard
# 5	2 yards
# 9	3 yards
# 12	1 yard

COLORS

greens	1 - 2 yards
pinks to reds	2 - 3 yards
purples to blues	1 - 2 yards
yellows to golds	1 - 2 yards

TIPS

- Some ribbons have only a subtle variation in the weave to differentiate between the right & wrong sides. Others, like the overdyed ribbons, are obvious. Use whichever side seems right for your project.

- French Ribbon may look fragile, but it is all right to wash and iron it. It is also dry cleanable; just remind your cleaners not to iron the flowers.

- Wrinkled ribbon or a kinked wire can be straightened by running it over the edge of a table to "iron" it. You can always undo an unsuccessful flower, lightly steam press the ribbon, and start over.

- The running stitches for gathering or ruching can vary from 1/32" to 1/4" in length. Just keep them even. When gathering into the center of a flower, longer stitches will result in a tighter center because the stitches will form big pleats rather than small gathers. Stitch a few inches; then gather it to see if you like the look. Remember that a center hole in a flower can always be filled or covered up.

- Gather the ribbon by holding the wire in one hand and pushing the ribbon back along it. Try not to angle the wire because this will tear the selvedge edge on some ribbons.

- Start by making one of each flower and leaf style. This will help you become comfortable with the ribbon. As your skills improve, you will want to try some of your own variations.

- Make quite a few flowers and leaves before you even consider the final arrangement. Then you'll be free to play with the shapes, sizes and colors.

- Save some of the pulled-out wire. It can be strung with beads or used to attach stamens. Also save ribbon scraps as small as 1/2", as they can be turned into buds or flower centers.

♪

Tightly
Gathered
Rose with
Cupped
Leaves

Full Blown
Gathered
Rose with
Large Leaves

Folded Rose
with Prairie
Point Leaves

Prairie Point Leaf

Ruched
Flower

Folded Bud

Large Leaf

Center Ruffled
Rosette with
Prairie Point
Leaves

Simple Rosette
with Bud
Centers and
Large Leaves

Cupped
Leaf

Looped leaf
or Blossom

Ruffled Bud

Roly-Poly Bud
or Berry

Double Rosette with Folded
Centers and Large Leaves

THE GATHERED ROSE

This is an easy-to-master flower which is gathered along the wires in the ribbon. The tightly gathered bud is lovely in all colors and kinds of ribbon. It can be either the main flower or a fill-in blossom. Expect each gathered rose to look slightly different, and don't be afraid to bend or crush it into a nice shape. One terrific full-blown rose is all you need for a dramatic brooch or as the focal point of a grouping. Go crazy and gather up 1 1/2 yds of # 9 ribbon, and your rose will be the talk of the town.

FULL BLOWN GATHERED ROSE YARDAGE

RIBBON SIZE	YARDAGE
#3	10"
#5	16"
#9	24"
#12	32"

DIRECTIONS

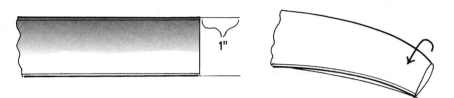

1. Gently and carefully push the ribbon back to expose 1" of both wires at one end of the ribbon.

2. Twist the wires together to anchor them.

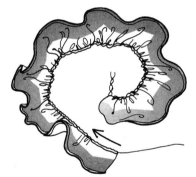

3. Push the ribbon along the wire to gather it tightly on the side you intend to be the flower center.

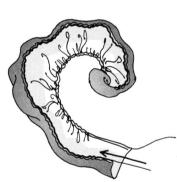

4. For the bud, also gather along the top edge until the top cups over.

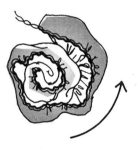

5. Roll up and wrap the bottom with the wire or stitch.

TIGHTLY GATHERED ROSE BUD YARDAGE

RIBBON SIZE	YARDAGE
#3	6"
#5	9"
#9	12"
#12	16"

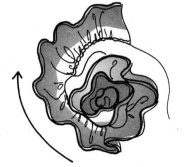

6. For the full-blown rose, follow Steps 1-3. Wind the ribbon around the center.

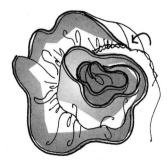

7. Push back the top edge of the ribbon so 1/2" of the wire is exposed. Twist the wires together and tuck the end under the rose.

DIRECTIONS

The folded rose is a colorful flower which shows off both edges of the ribbon. While the gathered rose looks like an old-fashioned blossom, this more geometric rendition resembles a modern hybrid. Although some people have trouble mastering this rose at first, once you catch on, you'll be able to turn out many flowers quickly and easily. Have your needle threaded, knotted, and ready to grab before beginning to fold. Some people wait until the flower is completely assembled to stitch it together at the bottom, but less nimble-fingered folk will prefer to take a stitch or two in the bottom after every few folds.

FULL BLOWN
FOLDED
ROSE
YARDAGE

RIBBON SIZE	YARDAGE
#3	10"
#5	16"
#9	24"
#12	32"

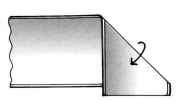

1. Fold over the raw edge of the ribbon at a 90° angle.

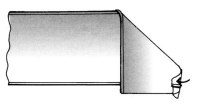

2. Begin rolling the ribbon at the right bottom point, forming a tail to hold onto.

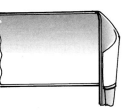

3. Roll the ribbon to the selvedge edge.

4. Fold back the ribbon at a 90° angle.

5. Roll again to the selvedge edge, coaxing the outer petal edge to flare out slightly.

6. For the bud, fold and roll twice. Take a small pleat about 1" from the end.

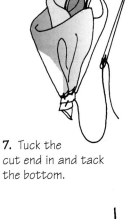

7. Tuck the cut end in and tack the bottom.

8. For the full blown rose, follow Steps 1-5. Continue rolling and folding back until the rose is full.

9. Tuck the cut end under.

10. Stitch the cut end and the bottom to secure them.

FOLDED
ROSE BUD
YARDAGE

RIBBON SIZE	YARDAGE
#3	2 1/2"
#5	4"
#9	6"
#12	8"

THE SIMPLE ROSETTE

RIBBON SIZE	YARDAGE
#3	6"
#5	8"
#9	12"
#12	16"

The simple rosette is an easy, less dimensional flower which can fill in the spaces behind or between more dramatic blooms. Try it in #3 & #5 ribbons for garments or miniature work. All the rosette variations are good choices when you want flowers which don't stick out very far off the surface. Rosettes look best in ombré ribbons, which really show off the color contrast between the center and the outer edge. Ombré blues are perfect for amazingly realistic morning glories to wind their way along a vest front or quilt border.

DIRECTIONS

1. Remove the wire from the edge of the ribbon which will become the flower center.

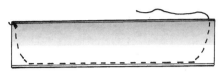

2. Sew a gathering stitch along the wireless edge, beginning and ending it near the other edge. Large stitches will result in a tighter center.

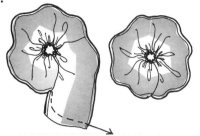

3. Gather the stitch tightly to form a circle. Overlap the ribbon ends and stitch closed.

4. If you end up with a hole in the center, cover it with a button or jewel, or fill it with a stuffed bud.

THE DOUBLE ROSETTE

RIBBON SIZE	YARDAGE	STITCHING DISTANCE FROM EDGE
#3	3"	1/4"
#5	4 1/2"	3/8"
#9	7"	1/2"
#12	9"	3/4"

If you stitch the double rosette from ombré ribbon, it will look as if two different ribbons were sewn together. Try two rosettes from the same ribbon, reversing the position of the dark edge. They'll be completely different flowers. Solid white or pink ribbon looks like hollyhocks. Ombré pink, with the light edge in the center, can be a rose of sharon if a dark stamen is added.

DIRECTIONS

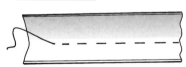

1. Run a gathering stitch.

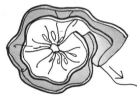

2. Gather the ribbon tightly, coaxing the narrow part to fold over the wider part.

3. Overlap the ends, hiding the raw edges behind the gathers, and stitch the ends in place. Fluff the rosette out a bit.

SUZANNE'S PANSY VARIATION

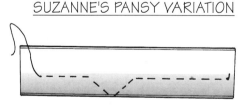

1. Run a gathering thread as in step 1 above, but stitch a point on the narrower side.

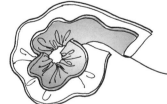

2. Gather the ribbon tightly, coaxing the narrow part to fold over the wider part.

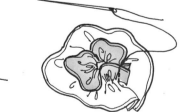

3. Using the gathering thread stitch together raw edges of the pansy "face".

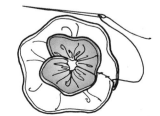

4. Fold under the remaining raw edges and tack.

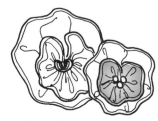

5. Add a yellow center.

This flower is a good example of how wonderful a mistake can be. A bit of overly enthusiastic gathering while attempting to make a double rosette led to this variation. It looks great in all sizes but is especially effective for miniature work because you get a lot of detail for a minimum of effort. Ombré ribbon helps emphasize the textural contrast of the center. Choose a range of yellows and oranges for a crop of marigolds, or stitch this rosette from shades of pink and red for carnations.

THE CENTER RUFFLED ROSETTE

RIBBON SIZE	YARDAGE	STITCHING DISTANCE FROM EDGE
#3	4 1/2"	1/4"
#5	8"	3/8"
#9	12"	5/8"
#12	15"	7/8"

DIRECTIONS

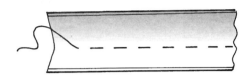

1. Stitch the ribbon as shown in Step 1 for the double rosette.

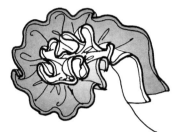

2. Gather the ribbon tightly, forcing the center to crinkle up.

3. Overlap and stitch the ends, fluffing the center into a crinkly texture.

4. Rosettes will look very different, depending on position of the dark edge.

DAFFODIL VARIATION

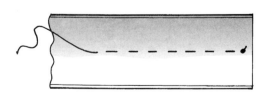

1. Run a gathering stitch down the exact center of a white, yellow, or orange solid or ombré ribbon.

2. Gather tightly and coax the center to stand up in a trumpet.

THE RUCHED FLOWER

EIGHT PETAL RUCHED FLOWER YARDAGE

RIBBON SIZE	YARDAGE
#3	6"
#5	8"
#9	12"
#12	16"

The ruched flower has been a popular and fashionable accessory since antebellum times. This versatile technique can also be used as a scalloped edging for garments and accessories. Eight petal flowers are the easiest to make. A double or even triple row of petals becomes a spectacular dahlia worthy of an heirloom Baltimore Album Quilt. The most realistic violets and primroses require six petals. They should be stitched with matching thread, as the gathering stitches will show a bit. Speed up the flower-making process by machine stitching the gathering lines. Use thread to match the flower color in the top and bobbin, loosening the upper thread tension and increasing the stitch length.

DIRECTIONS

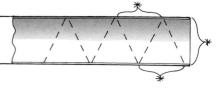

1. The space between the legs of the zigzag gathering line should be equal to the width of your ribbon.

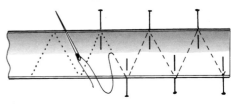

2. Start by measuring and pin marking. Run a tiny, even gathering stitch. After stitching a few inches, you can then eyeball it.

3. Pull up the gathers until the ribbon is half its original length. Knot off to secure. Even out the gathers.

4. Curve the ribbon around so the inner scallops touch. Tack the scallops together in the center

VARIATIONS

1. <u>A Multi-Layered Flower:</u> Spiral the ruching so the second layer is behind the first. Tack.

2. <u>A Three-Dimensional Center:</u> Gather up more tightly. Curve up the inner scallops to form a 3-D center. Tack.

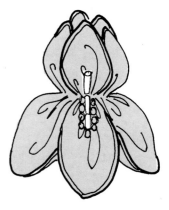

3. <u>An Iris:</u> Bend the center up and the outer petals down. Add gold and purple beads to form the iris beard.

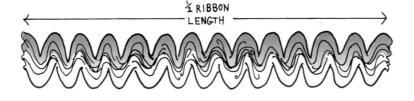

½ RIBBON LENGTH

4. <u>Ruched Scallop Trimming:</u> Measure the length of the area to be trimmed. Cut the ribbon twice this length. Gather to fit.

Save all the short ends of ribbon for buds. We like to scatter two or three among the full-bloom roses. Try stuffing one in the center of a rosette for a more dimensional accent.

If you gather together a group of ribbons in rich shades of purples and wines, the result will be a luscious bunch of grapes. Our friend Sally created a lovely thistle head by stitching up the ruffled bud variation from green-to-lavender ombré ribbon. For a firm bud, use Morning Glory's Old Fashion Cotton Stuffing, which holds its shape nicely.

THE ROLY-POLY BUD OR BERRY

BUD OR BERRY YARDAGE

RIBBON SIZE	YARDAGE
#3	2"
#5	3"
#9	4 1/2"
#12	6"

DIRECTIONS

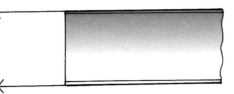

1. Remove the wires from both sides of the ribbon.

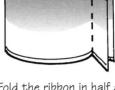

2. Fold the ribbon in half and stitch the cut ends together using 1/4" seams.

3. Turn the ribbon right side out and finger press.

4. Run a gathering stitch right below the top selvedge edge.

5. Pull the gathers tightly and stitch it closed.

6. Run a gathering stitch along the bottom edge

7. Firmly stuff the bud.

8. Pull the bottom thread to close up the bud.

RUFFLED BUD VARIATIONS

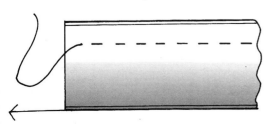

1. Leave the wire in the top of the ribbon but remove it from the bottom. Run a gathering stitch 1/4 of the way down from the top edge of the ribbon.

2. Follow Steps 5 to 8 above.

THE PRAIRIE POINT LEAF

PRAIRIE POINT LEAF YARDAGE

RIBBON SIZE	YARDAGE
#3	1 1/2"
#5	2 1/2"
#9	3 1/2"
#12	4 1/2"

The prairie point leaf should be made from ribbon the same size or wider than the flower it accompanies. Make many more leaves than you expect to need, so they'll be ready to tuck into bare spaces among the flowers. Use every shade of green you can find plus rusts, turquoises, reds, purples, even gold and silver. Form this leaf from pinks and blues and, voila! -- you have flower petals!

DIRECTIONS

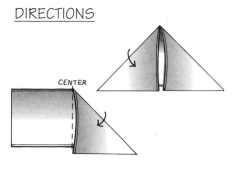 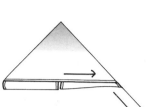 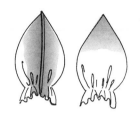 

1. Fold the ribbon to form a prairie point.

2. If you like, pull out the bottom wire.

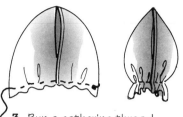

3. Run a gathering thread across the bottom of the folded ribbon. Take a few stitches to hold it in place.

4. Either side of the leaf can face upward.

5. Be sure to tuck the raw edges under the flowers where they won't show.

THE CUPPED LEAF OR PETAL

The small cupped leaf works well as a fill-in under roses or delicate flower petals. The large leaf is a dead ringer for a geranium petal. Two or three large leaves are all you need to cover the hardware for a pin or barrette.

SMALL CUPPED LEAF YARDAGE

RIBBON SIZE	YARDAGE
#3	2 1/2"
#5	3 1/2"
#9	5"
#12	7"

LARGE CUPPED LEAF YARDAGE

RIBBON SIZE	YARDAGE
#3	4"
#5	7 1/2"
#9	10"
#12	15"

DIRECTIONS

1. Gather one side of the ribbon by gently and evenly pulling from each end of the wire. Be sure to hold onto both ends of the wire while gathering, or you'll accidentally pull it out.

2. Gather the ribbon as tightly as possible. Twist the wires to hold.

3. Pull the loose top ends down to meet the gathered bottom. The ribbon will cup over.

 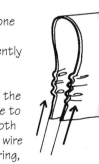  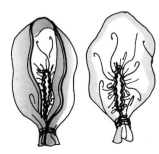

4. Wrap the ends of the wire around the bottom.

5. Either side of the leaf may face up

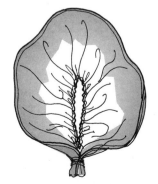

6. The large leaf is made the same way, but it will flatten and flare out more.

Sometimes a long fill-in shape is needed to set off the rest of the predominantly round and oval leaves and blossoms. Green ribbons are a natural for foliage. Try a palette of pinks, reds, and purples for easy snapdragons or blues and lavenders for delphinium.

3 LOOP LEAF & BLOSSOM YARDAGE

RIBBON SIZE	YARDAGE
#3	10"
#5	11"
#9	16"
#12*	18"

*(#12 needs two tucks at the bottom)

DIRECTIONS

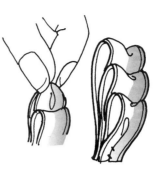

1. Fold the ribbon, making three progressively larger loops.

2. Fold a tuck in the bottom and stitch through all three loops.

3. Pinch the top of each loop together to form a dimple.

VARIATIONS

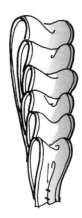

1. <u>Shading:</u> Fold as in Step 1, twisting the ombré ribbon at the bottom of each loop so the shading changes sides.

2. <u>Snapdragon:</u> Use #3 ribbon and fold six loops instead of three.

FLOWER PETAL VARIATIONS

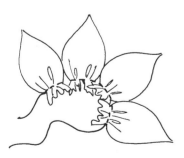

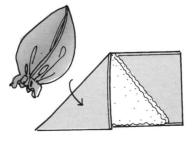

1. Machine stitch a string of prairie point leaves together and gather them into a flower.

2. For a plump rose bud, fold a triangular scrap of batting into a red or pink prairie point.

3. Overlap four or five cupped petals. Cover the center with a button.

GILDING THE LILY

A button, a sequin or a few beads may be just what you need to turn your ribbon flowers into a real work of art. Sew on your embellishments with beading thread or sewing thread in a color to match the beads.

A button or sew-on jewel is a good flower center. It can also hide not-so-neat tacking stitches.

Try sewing on large sequins using contrasting color thread.

Nestle beads inside a center ruffled rosette.

Beads can dress up plain flowers & leaves and catch the light.

Add a few gold & purple beads for a more realistic pansy.

String beads on wires to create a dimensional center. Great for hats & jewelry!

Tie a loose knot in a short piece of ribbon.

Stuff into the center of a rosette.

Small stuffed buds are great flower centers.

DIRECTIONS FOR ROLLED FLOWER CENTER

1. Cut a 1/2" to 2" scrap of ribbon.

2. Fold so selvedges meet.

3. Fold the cut edges into the center.

4. Repeat until you have a nice tight center.

5. Stuff into the flower.

*W*arm firelight tones are reminiscent of a bouquet of dried flowers. Rejuvenate a favorite sweater by adding new buttons along with the ruched ribbons.

PINS

A pin is an easy first project. One rose surrounded by leaves can add a feminine touch to a tailored suit. Or try putting together a cluster of smaller blooms in shades which coordinate with your favorite print dress or skirt. For a dressier look, add a few beads to the leaves or inner flower petals.

SUPPLIES FOR A SINGLE ROSE PIN

One large gathered rose from #9 ribbon

Seven leaves from #9 ribbon

3" circle of stiff crinoline

3" circle of Ultrasuede®, leather, or felt

1 1/4" pin back

Dark or light beading thread to match flowers

Optional beads

DIRECTIONS

1. If you're adding beads, sew them onto the flowers and leaves first.

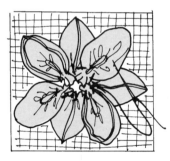

2. Stitch the leaves, then the flowers onto the crinoline, keeping them in a tight cluster. Use beading or heavier thread and a Milliners needle. Use stitches to tack the flowers in place.

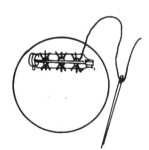

3. Trim away the excess crinoline so it doesn't show from the front.

4. Trim the Ultrasuede® so it's slightly larger than the crinoline. Stitch the pin back to the Ultrasuede®, positioning it near the top edge.

5. Sew the Ultrasuede® to the crinoline, catching the underside of the leaves to help them lie flat.

You may find yourself making several versions of this easy-to-assemble bag. Stitch it up in velvet, brocade or bengaline (moiré faille) for evening. Enlarge the pattern slightly and choose denim, Ultrasuede® or a handwoven ethnic fabric for a more casual bag. We usually sew the flowers to the bag before assembling it, but you can tack them in place after it is sewn together if you prefer. We often like to finish the edge with cord or piping.

SUPPLIES

Fabric: 1/2 yd. or one fat quarter for outside and lining
Stiff interfacing: 1/4 yd.
Sewing thread to match fabric
Cord: 1 yd., 1/4" to 3/8" in diameter for handle
6 to 11 flowers and 10 to 14 leaves
Crinoline to back the flower groupings
Large covered snap for closure
Optional: beads and buttons for embellishment
Optional: 9" x12" piece of stiff crinoline (if you like a stiff bag)

DIRECTIONS

1. Cut out one lining and one outside section, each 8" x 20". Use the curved pattern on this page for the curve of the flap.

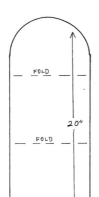

2. Fuse the interfacing to the lining.

3. Arrange the flowers on the bag flap using one of the basic formats shown here. Sew the flower and leaf groupings to the crinoline. Trim the crinoline so it doesn't show; then sew the groups to the flap.

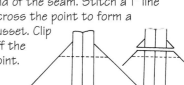

4. Cut the optional stiff crinoline without a seam allowances and pin it to the wrong side of the lining. Fold up the main body of the bag, right sides together. Sew the side seams to within 1/4" of the top edge.

5. Snip the seam fold right up to the stitching.

CLIP

6. Press open each seam. Flatten out the bag to form a point at the end of the seam. Stitch a 1" line across the point to form a gusset. Clip off the point.

7. Sew the lining together following Steps 1-5; then sew the lining and bag right sides together at the flap.

8. Grade and clip the seam, turn right side out, and gently press the flap.

9. Push the lining inside the bag. Sew a large snap or velcro dot to the bag front and flap.

10. Turn the top edges in and blind stitch them closed.

*J*ewel toned flowers add an elegant and sophisticated note of color to a simple jacket and hat. Two or three pins can be clustered on the jacket, or worn separately.

Strong blues and yellows are traditional Country French colors. A casual ticking-striped vest takes on a carnival air when ribbons are used as a linear element to offset the brightly colored rosettes.

SMALL ACCESSORIES

Good things really do come in small packages. Many ready-to-finish items are just waiting to be transformed into special gifts for yourself and your favorite people.

NECKLACES

A length of fancy cord is all you need to turn a pretty flower pin into a necklace. Follow our directions for assembling a pin, but sandwich the hanging cord between the crinoline and the Ultrasuede® backing. Glue or stitch it securely in place.

Another method is to use a pendant form such as Pat and Pam's Creative Charms, which snaps together like a covered button. Trace the form's outline on the wrong side of the fabric and thread baste over the markings. Arrange and stitch down the flowers. Trim the fabric down to a 3/4" allowance. Snap it into the form, and you're ready to hang the pendant on a chain or cord.

BARRETTES & COMBS

Plain barrettes and combs are available in most craft stores. Start your arrangement with a base of leaves which will cover the hardware. The large ruffled leaves seem to be made just for this purpose. Stitch the foliage and flowers onto stiff crinoline; then stitch or glue the crinoline to the barrette or comb.

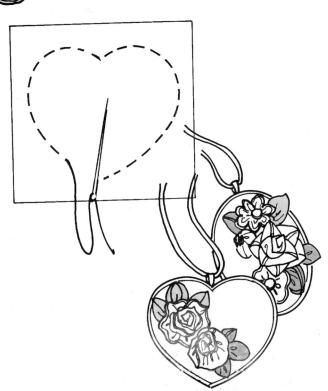

BOXES & JARS

Adorn your home with ribbon flowers.
Many needlework or quilt shops carry
wooden or porcelain boxes or jars, like
the Framecraft® jar shown on the color
pages. Or look for frame forms, hat
boxes, and hand mirrors just waiting to be
covered in fabric and embellished with
handmade blossoms.
Study the color photos
for ideas to get you
started.

PIN CUSHIONS

Pin cushions are easy and fun to make.
Aside from the obvious function of holding
pins and needles, a very special one can sit
on a dresser displaying your favorite pieces
of jewelry.

To assemble the pin cushion, stitch
it together, then turn it right side out and
pin the flowers in place. Try rolling the pin
cushion over your hand, or stuff a large
handful of cotton stuffing inside to get an
idea of how it will look fully stuffed. You
may find you need to cluster the flowers
closer together. Sew the flowers in place;
then stuff. Diane likes to sew 1/4 to 1/2 cup
lead shot into a small "pillowcase" shaped
like the pincushion and place it in the
bottom of the cushion before stuffing. This
gives the pin cushion a stable base. For an
elegant finish, tack a strip of ruched ribbon
around the edge of the
pin cushion.

*M*enswear
pinstripes and denim
take on a completely
different feeling
when they are
dressed up with
the bright
midsummer colors
of morning glories
and hollyhocks.

24

HATS

Hats used to be the final elegant and necessary finish for all well-dressed women. We'd like to encourage the wearing of hats. If your life doesn't include many hat wearing opportunities, perhaps it's time to stage an occasion or two. Meet your friends at an elegant downtown hotel for high tea. Host a hat and glove luncheon for a visiting relative. One monthly quilt club meeting might include a prize for the member sporting the prettiest or most original hat. If all else fails, hang your creation on the wall or on a door and enjoy it every day.

Everyone will choose a different style of hat, which is just fine. Here are a few tips and ideas which can be adapted for your favorite chapeau.

If you'd rather not sew the flowers directly to the hat, stitch the floral groupings to crinoline, then sew them to a ribbon. You might choose a band of ombré French ribbon, a more sedate velvet ribbon, or grosgrain in the same shade as the hat. Tack the band right through the hat, using thread which matches the band.

Add loops, a bow, or streamers to accent the flowers. If traditional horizontal bow loops don't suit your hat, try fanning them out above or below the flowers. The cockade, a circular arrangement of loops or points, was a popular hat decoration in past times. It's a good base for a cluster of flowers. Elegance French wire-edged ribbons are fun to work with because you can easily coax them into shape.

Audition more than one arrangement of flowers and loops before making a final choice.

A bridal wreath of roses in ombré taffeta and sheer organdy ribbons will be treasured and passed down to the next lucky bride. A matching pin or comb is a lovely remembrance for each bridesmaid.

What could be more romantic than roses and pansies in rich Victorian hues? Set them off with the luxurious textures of velvet and moiré.

VESTS

The ideas shown here as vests are easy to adapt to other wearables. If you don't enjoy sewing garments, revive a favorite old sweater or hit the sales for a new jacket or blouse to embellish.

TIPS FOR DESIGNING A BEAUTIFUL VEST

- Consider making your vest from fabric with a bit of texture to make the unadorned expanses of the vest more interesting. A dressy vest could be velvet, brocade, or bengaline (moiré faille). For a more casual style, homespun, wool tweed, or small monochromatic cotton prints are all good choices.

- Strive for variety within your chosen color scheme. Include pinks ranging from peachy shades to orchid pinks. Blue flowers might start with watery aquas and slide all the way into lavender or violet tones.

- Vary the size and shape of the flowers and leaves as well. Even if you are just crazy about roses, add a few crinkly-centered rosettes or stuffed buds to the group. They will help underscore the beauty of the roses. Try more than one arrangement. Photos allow you to compare different arrangements, and they will often accentuate an awkward area or blossom which you might not "see" in person. Take Polaroids or run regular film down to the one-hour photo lab.

- Keep the flowers in scale with your body. Tall people are able to carry off clusters of large roses or ruched daisies. Shorter, small-boned people will want to concentrate on more delicate-looking blossoms. Most of us will fall somewhere in between.

- Try not to draw attention to problem areas of the body. Avoid circling your hips with full-blown roses, and, please - no matching ruched dahlias like pasties on each vest front!

- Create a graceful line with the flowers. The illustrations show some easy-to-follow guidelines for floral groupings. Notice how they undulate, becoming wider and narrower to accommodate differing sizes or numbers of flowers.

- It's not necessary to make any permanent placement markings on your garment. Mark the fronts with straight pins to make temporary guidelines which will help position the flowers. Or you might wish to try the technique shown on the pink and light blue vests: sew several overlapping, curving lines using decorative machine stitches. Then sew the flowers along the lines.

- Diagonal lines, as shown in this illustration, are flattering to all body types. Plan to wear the vest buttoned so the design flows nicely across the front.

- Asymmetrical designs are more eye-catching than two mirror-image front halves. If you don't feel confident in balancing an extremely asymmetrical design, try this - change the position, size, or color of some flowers so the two front sections are slightly different.

- Your favorite vest pattern (We've used Quilter's Resource Inc.'s Versatile Vests.)
- Vest fabric and lining (Check the pattern for yardage.)
- Interfacing for the neckline and front closure area (Flannel works well.) If the vest fabric is flimsy, we suggest fusing lightweight interfacing to the fabric before you cut it out.
- Buttons or closures
- Completed flowers and leaves (Study the photos to get an idea of how many you might need.)
- Optional: shiny threads or fancy yarns for decorative lines

DIRECTIONS

1. Cut out all vest and lining pieces. Sew the vest together at the shoulders.

2. If you plan to add decorative lines, pin-mark them one at a time and sew.

3. Assemble the vest and lining. If you plan to bind the edges, trim them to size, but don't bind the vest until you've sewn on the flowers.

4. Pin the vest up on a board or put it on a dressmaker's form. Arrange the flower groupings. Try the vest on to be sure you like the placement.

5. Stitch the groupings to crinoline. Trim the crinoline so it doesn't show from the front.

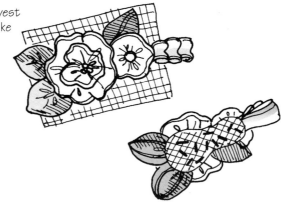

6. Sew the groupings to the vest, but take care not to stitch through the lining.

7. Bind the vest. Wear you new creation and enjoy the compliments!

*M*asses of roses in every possible shade of pink are perfect for a very feminine vest. Textured brocades add interest to the unadorned parts of the vest and bag.

This delicate vest sports smaller and fewer flowers in a springtime palette inspired by delphinium and pansies. Curving lines of machine stitches carry the colors down the front.

Dressing table accessories are always welcome gifts. Purple moiré is a good background for pansies and rosettes centered with vintage pearl buttons.

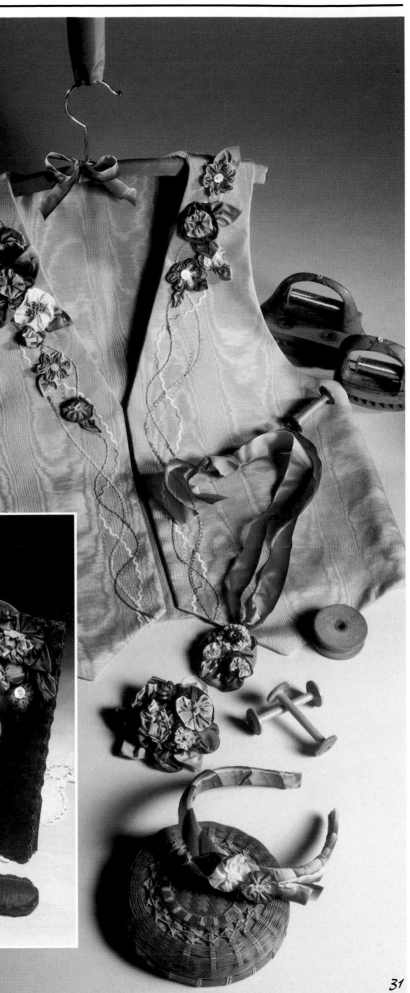

SHOES

Attention all shoe-shopping junkies! Now you really can tiptoe through the tulips! Imagine fuschia buds on black satin T straps to coordinate with a favorite evening dress, white wedding slippers crowned with pale roses, or tailored black rosettes on simple black pumps. Bridesmaids no longer have to settle for plain dyed-to-match shoes. Teenage prom-goers can bring new meaning to the term "happy feet."

It's easy to stitch through most fabric shoes. A trip to the shoe store may produce a wealth of likely candidates: canvas high-tops, velvet flats, linen mary janes, or strappy sandals. If you'd prefer to temporarily dress up a good pair of leather shoes, many craft stores and shoe repair shops carry plain shoe clips.

Here's what you need to make a pair of pretty shoes like the velvet flats shown on the color pages.

SUPPLIES

- 3 flowers: either tightly gathered buds made from #9 or #5 ribbon, or full blown gathered or folded roses made from #5 ribbon
- 3 leaves made from #9 ribbon
- Crinoline for backing
- Beading thread for tacking
- Optional: shoe clips

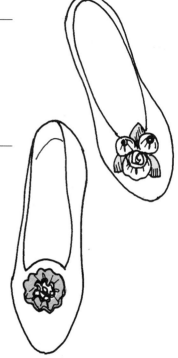

DIRECTIONS

1. Sew leaves and then flowers to crinoline. Trim the crinoline so it won't show.

2. Tack the crinoline base to the shoe, or...

3. Sew or glue the crinoline-backed flowers to shoe clips

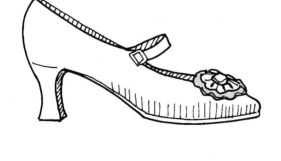